Mary White Rowlandson

A Narrative of the Captivity, Sufferings, and Removes, of

Mrs. Mary Rowlandson

Who was taken prisoner by the Indians. With several others.

Mary White Rowlandson

A Narrative of the Captivity, Sufferings, and Removes, of Mrs. Mary Rowlandson
Who was taken prisoner by the Indians. With several others.

ISBN/EAN: 9783744794442

Printed in Europe, USA, Canada, Australia, Japan

Cover: Foto ©ninafisch / pixelio.de

More available books at **www.hansebooks.com**

A
NARRATIVE

OF THE

Captivity, Sufferings, and Removes,

OF

Mrs. *Mary Rowlandson,*

Who was taken Prisoner by the *Indians ;* with several
others ; and treated in the most barbarous and cruel
Manner by those vile *Savages :* With many other
remarkable Events during her Travels.

*Written by her own Hand, for her private Use, and since
made public at the earnest Desire of some Friends, and for
the Benefit of the Afflicted.*

BOSTON:
Re-printed and sold by Thomas and John Fleet, at the
Bible and Heart, Cornhill, 1791.

A
NARRATIVE
OF THE
Captivity and Removes
OF
Mrs. *Mary Rowlandfon.*

ON t'e 10th of *February,* 1675, came the *Indians* with great numbers upon *Lancafter* : their firſt coming was about fun-riſing ; hearing the noiſe of ſome guns, we looked out : ſeveral houſes were burning, and the ſmoke aſcending to heaven. There were five perſons taken in one houſe, the father and mother, and a ſucking child they knocked on the head, the other two they took and carried away alive. There were two others, who being out of their garriſon upon occaſion, were ſet upon ; one was knocked on the head, the other eſcaped: Another there was who running along was ſhot and wounded, and fell down ; he begged of them his life, promiſing them money (as they told me) but they would not hearken to him, but knocked him on the head, ſtript him naked, and ſplit open his bowels. Another ſeeing many of the *Indians* about his barn, ventur'd and went out, but was quickly ſhot down. There were three others belonging to the ſame garriſon who were killed; the *Indians* getting up upon the roof of the barn, had advantage to ſhoot down upon them over their fortification. Thus theſe murtherous wretches went on burning & deſtroying all before them.

At length they came and beſet our houſe, and quickly it was the dolefuleſt day that ever mine eyes ſaw. The houſe ſtood upon the edge of a hill ; ſome of the *Indians* got behind the hill, others into the barn, and others behind any thing that would ſhelter them ; from all which places they ſhot againſt the houſe, ſo that the bullets ſeemed to fly like hail, and quickly they wounded one man among us, then another, and then a third. About two hours (according to my obſervation in that amazing time) they had been

about

about the houſe before they prevail'd to fire it, (which they did with flax and hemp which they brought out of the barn, and there being no defence about the houſe, only two flankers at two oppoſite corners, and one of them not finiſhed) they fired it once, and one ventured out and quenched it, but they quickly fired it again, and that took   Now is the dreadful hour come, that I have often heard of (in time of the war, as it was the caſe of others) but now mine eyes ſee it.   Some in our houſe were fighting for their lives, others wallowing in blood, the houſe on fire over our heads, and the bloody heathen ready to knock us on the head if we ſtirred out   Now might we hear mothers and children crying out for themſelves and one onother, *Lord, what ſhall we do !* Then I took my children (and one of my ſiſters her's) to go forth and leave the houſe: but as ſoon as we came to the door, and appear'd, the *Indians* ſhot ſo thick, that the bullets rattled againſt the houſe, as if one had taken a handful of ſtones and threw them, ſo that we were forced to give back.   We had ſix ſtout dogs belonging to our garriſon, but none of them would ſtir, though at another time, if an *Indian* had come to the door, they were ready to fly upon him and tear him down. The Lord hereby would make us the more to acknowledge his hand, and to ſee that our help is always in him.   But out we muſt go, the fire increaſing, and coming along behind us roaring, and the *Indians* gaping before us with their guns, ſpears, and hatchets to devour us.   No ſooner were we out of the houſe, but my brother-in-law (being before wounded in defending the houſe, in or near the throat) fell down dead, whereat the *Indians* ſcornfully ſhouted and hallowed, and were preſently upon him, ſtripping off his cloaths   The bullets flying thick, one went through my ſide, and the ſame (as would ſeem) through the bowels and hand of my poor child in my arms.   One of my elder ſiſter's children (named *William*) had then his leg broke, which the *Indians* perceiving, they knocked him on the head.   Thus were we butchered by thoſe merciless heathens, ſtanding amazed, with the blood running down to our heels.   My eldeſt ſiſter being yet in the houſe, and ſeeing thoſe woeful ſights, the infidels halling mothers one way and children another, and ſome wallowing in their blood : And her eldeſt ſon telling her that her ſon *William* was dead, and myſelf was wounded, ſhe ſaid, and *Lord let me die with them* : which was no ſooner ſaid, but ſhe was ſtruck with a bullet, and fell down dead over the threſhold.   I hope ſhe is reaping the fruit of her good labours, being faithful to the ſervice of God in her place.   In her younger years ſhe lay under much trouble upon ſpiritual accounts, till it pleaſed God to make that precious ſcripture take hold of her heart, *2 Cor.* 12. 9. *And he ſaid unto me, My grace is ſufficient for thee.*
                                                             More

More than twenty years after, I have heard her tell how sweet and comfortable that place was to her. But to return ; The *Indians* laid hold of us, pulling me one way, and the children another, and said, *Come, go along with us* : I told them they would kill me ; they answered, *If I were willing to go along with them, they would not hurt me.*

Oh! the doleful sight that now was to behold at this house ! Come behold the works of the Lord, what desolations he has made in the earth. Of thirty-seven persons who were in this one house, none escaped either present death, or a bitter captivity, save only one, who might say as in *Job* 1, 15. *And I only am escaped alone to tell the news.* There were twelve killed, some shot, some stabbed with their spears, some knocked down with their hatchets. When we are in prosperity, Oh the little that we think of such dreadful fights, to see our dear friends and relations lie bleeding out their hearts-blood upon the ground. There was one who was chopt in the head with a hatchet, and stript naked, and yet was crawling up and down. It was a solemn sight to see so many christians lying in their blood, some here and some there, like a company of sheep torn by wolves. All of them stript naked by a company of hell-hounds, roaring, singing, ranting and insulting, as if they would have torn our very hearts out; yet the Lord by his almighty power, preserved a number of us from death, for there were twenty-four of us taken alive and carried captive.

I had often before this said, that if the *Indians* should come, I should chuse rather to be killed by them, than taken alive · but when it came to the trial, my mind changed; their glittering weapons so daunted my spirit, that I chose rather to go along with those (as I may say) ravenous bears, than that moment to end my days. And that I may the better declare what happened to me during that grievous captivity, I shall particularly speak of the several Removes we had up and down the wilderness.

The first Remove.

NOW away we must go with those barbarous creatures, with our bodies wounded and bleeding, and our hearts no less than our bodies. About a mile we went that night, up upon a hill within sight of the town, where we intended to lodge. There was hard by a vacant house (deserted by the *English* before, for fear of the *Indians*) I asked them whether I might not lodge in the house that night ? to which they answered, What, will you love *Englishmen* still ? This was the dolefulest night that ever my eyes saw. Oh the roaring, and singing, and dancing, and yelling of
those

those black creatures in the night, which made the place a lively resemblance of hell : And miserable was the waste that was there made. of horses. cattle, sheep, swine, calves, lambs, roasting pigs and fowls (which they had plundered in the town) some roasting. some lying and burning, and some boiling, to feed our merciless enemies : who were joyful enough, though we were disconsolate. To add to the dolefulness of the former day, and the dismalness of the present night, my thoughts ran upon my losses and sad bereaved condition. All was gone, my husband gone, (at least separated from me, he being in the *Bay* ; and to add to my grief, the *Indians* told me they would kill him as he came homeward) my children gone, my relations and friends gone our house and home, and all our comforts within door and without. all was gone (except my life) and I knew not but the next moment that might go too.

There remained nothing to me but one poor wounded babe, and it seemed at present worse than death, that it was in such a pitiful condition, bespeaking compassion, and I had no refreshing for it, nor suitable things to revive it. Little do many think what is the savageness and brutishness of this barbarous enemy, those even that seem to profess more than others among them, when the *English* have fallen into their hands.

Those seven that were killed at *Lancaster* the summer before upon a sabbath day, and the one that was afterward killed upon a week day, were slain and mangled in a barbarous manner, by one-ey'd *John*. and *Marlborough*'s praying *Indians*, which Capt. *Mosely* brought to *Boston*, as the *Indians* told me.

The second Remove.

BUT now (the next morning) I must turn my back upon the town, and travel with them into the vast and desolate wilderness, I know not whither. It is not my tongue or pen can express the sorrows of my heart, and bitterness of my spirit, that I had at this departure : But God was with me in a wonderful manner, carrying me along. and bearing up my spirit, that it did not quite fail. One of the *Indians* carried my poor wounded babe upon a horse ; it went moaning all along, *I shall die, I shall die.* I went on foot after it, with sorrow that cannot be exprest. At length I took it off the horse, and carried it in my arms till my strength failed, and I fell down with it. Then they set me upon a horse, with my wounded child in my lap, and there being no furniture upon the horse's back. as we were going down a steep hill, we both fell over the horse's head, at which they like inhuman crea-

tures

tures laughed, and rejoiced to fee it, though I thought we ſhould there have ended our days, overcome with ſo many difficulties. But the Lord renewed my ſtrength ſtill, and carry'd me along, that I might fee more of his power, yea ſo much that I could never have thought of, had I not experienced it.

After this it quickly began to ſnow, and when night came on, they ſtopt: and now down I muſt fit in the ſnow, by a little fire, and a few boughs behind me, with my ſick child in my lap, and calling much for water, being now (through the wound) fallen into a violent fever. My own wound alſo growing ſo ſtiff, that I could ſcarce fit down or riſe up, yet ſo it muſt be, that I muſt fit all this cold winter night, upon the cold ſnowy ground, with my ſick child in my arms, looking that every hour would be the laſt of Its life ; and having no chriſtian friend near me, either to comfort or help me. Oh I may fee the wonderful power of God, that my ſpirit did not utterly ſink under my affliction ; ſtill the Lord upheld me with his gracious and merciful ſpirit, and we were both alive to fee the light of the next morning.

The third Remove.

THE morning being come, they prepared to go on their way, one of the *Indians* got upon a horſe, and they ſat me up behind him, with my poor ſick babe in my lap, A very weariſome and tedious day I had of it ; what with my own wound, and my child being ſo exceeding ſick, and in a lamentable condition with her wound, it may eaſily be judged what a poor feeble condition we were in, there being not the leaſt crumb of refreſhing that came within either of our mouths from *Wedneſday* night to *Saturday* night, except only a little cold water. This day in the afternoon, about an hour by ſun, we came to the place where they intended, *viz.* an *Indian* town called *Wenimeſſet*, northward of *Quabaug*. When we were come, Oh the number of *Pagans* (now merciless enemies) that there came about me, that I may ſay as *David*, P .. 7. 13, *I had fainted, unleſs I had believed*, &c. The next day was the ſabbath : I then remembered how careleſs I had been of Gods holy time : how many ſabbaths I had loſt and miſſpent, and how evilly I had walked in God's ſight ; which lay ſo cloſe upon my ſpirit, that it was eaſy for me to fee how righteous it was with God to cut off the thread of my life, and caſt me out of his preſence forever. Yet the Lord ſtill ſhewed mercy to me, and helped me ; and as he wounded me with one hand, ſo he healed me with the other. This day there came to me one *Robert Pepper* (a man belonging to *Roxbury*) who was taken at Capt. *Beers*'s fight ; and had been now a conſiderable time with the *Indians*, and up with

them

them almost as far as *Albany*, to see King *Philip*, as he told me, and was now very lately come with them into these parts. Hearing, I say, that I was in this *Indian* town, he obtained leave to come and see me. He told me he himself was wounded in the leg, at Capt. *Beers's* fight; and was not able some time to go, but as they carried him, and that he took oak leaves and laid to his wound, and by the blessing of God, he was able to travel again. Then took I oak leaves and laid to my side, and with the blessing of God, it cured me also; yet before the cure was wrought, I may say as it is in *Psal.* 38. 5, 6. *My wounds stink and are corrupt, I am troubled, I am bowed down greatly, I go mourning all the day long.* I sat much alone with my poor wounded child in my lap, which moaned night and day, having nothing to revive the body, or chear the spirits of her; but instead of that, one *Indian* would come and tell me one hour, your master will knock your child on the head, and then a second, and then a third, your master will quickly knock your child on the head.

This was the comfort I had from them; miserable comforters were they all. Thus nine days I sat upon my knees, with my babe in my lap, till my flesh was raw again. My child being even ready to depart this sorrowful world, they bid me carry it out to another wigwam: (I suppose because they would not be troubled with such spectacles) whither I went with a very heavy heart, and down I sat with the picture of death in my lap. About two hours in the night, my sweet babe like a lamb departed this life, on *Feb.* 18. 1675, it being about six years and five months old. It was nine days from the first wounding, in this miserable condition, without any refreshing of one nature or another, except a little cold water. I cannot but take notice, how at another time I could not bear to be in a room where a dead person was, but now the case is changed; I must and could lie down with my dead babe all the night after. I have thought since of the wonderful goodness of God to me, in preserving me so in the use of my reason and senses, in that distressed time, that I did not use wicked and violent means to end my own miserable life. In the morning, when they understood that my child was dead, they sent me home to my master's wigwam: (By my master in this writing, must be understood *Quannopin*, who was a Saggamore, and married King *Philip's* wife's sister; not that he first took me, but I was sold to him by a *Narraganset Indian*, who took me when I first came out of the garrison) I went to take up my dead child in my arms to carry it with me, but they bid me let it alone: There was no resisting, but go I must, and leave it. When I had been awhile at my master's wigwam, I took the first opportunity I could get, to go look after my dead child: When I came I
asked

asked them what they had done with it? they told me it was on the hill;
then they went and shewed me where it was, where I saw the ground
was newly digged, and where they told me they had buried it; there
I left that child in the wilderness, and must commit it and my self
also in this wilderness condition, to him who is above all. God
having taken away this dear child, I went to see my daughter
Mary, who was at the same *Indian* town, at a wigwam not very
far off, though we had little liberty or opportunity to see one another; she was about ten years old, and taken from the door at
first by a praying *Indian*, and afterwards sold for a gun. When I
came in sight she would fall a weeping, at which they were pro-
voked, and would not let me come near her, but bid me be gone;
which was a heart-cutting word to me. I had one child dead, another in the wilderness, I knew not where, the third they would not
let me come near to; *Me (as he said) have ye bereaved of my childrens
Joseph is not, and Simeon is not, and ye will take Benjamin also,
all these things are against me* I could not sit still in this condition,
but kept walking from one place to another. And as I was going
along, my heart was even overwhelmed with the thoughts of my
condition, and that I should have children, and a nation that I knew
not ruled over them. Whereupon I earnestly entreated the Lord
that he would consider my low estate, and shew me a token for
good, and if it were his blessed will, some sign and hope of some
relief. And indeed quickly the Lord answered in some measure,
my poor prayer: For as I was going up and down mourning and
lamenting my condition, my son came to me and asked me how he
did? I had not seen him before since the destruction of the town;
and I knew not where he was, till I was informed by himself, that
he was amongst a smaller parcel of *Indians*, whose place was about
six miles off, with tears in his eyes he asked me whether his sister
Sarah was dead? and told me he had seen his sister *Mary*; and
prayed me, that I would not be troubled in reference to himself. The
occasion of his coming to see me at this time was this: There
was, as I said, about six miles from us a small plantation of *Indians*,
where it seems he had been during his captivity; and at this time,
there were some forces of the *Indians* gathered out of our company,
and some also from them (amongst whom was my son's master) to
go to assault and burn *Medfield*: In his time of his master's absence,
his dame brought him to see me. I took this to be some gracious
answer to my earnest and unfeigned desire. The next day the Indians returned from *Medfield*: (all the company, for those that be-
longed to the other smaller company, came through the town that
now we were at) but before they came to us. Oh the outragous
roaring and hooping that there was! they began their din about

a mile before they came to us, By their noife and hooping they fignified how many they had deftroyed; which was at that time twenty-three. Thofe that were with us at home, were gathered together as foon as they heard the hooping and every time that the other went over their number, thefe at home gave a fhout, that the very earth rang again. And thus they continued till thofe that had been upon the expedition were come up to the Saggamore's wig-wam; and then Oh the hideous infulting and triumphing that there was over fome *English* mens fcalps, that they had taken (as their manner is) and brought with them. I cannot but take notice of the wonderful mercy of God to me in thofe afflictions, in fending me a *Bible*: One of the *Indians* that came from *Medfield* fight, and had brought fome plunder, came to me, and afked me if I would have a *Bible*, he had got one in his bafket, I was glad of it, and afked him if he thought the *Indians* would let me read? he anfwer-ed yes; fo I took the *Bible*, and in that melancholy time, it came into my mind to read firft the 28 chap. of *Deuteronomy*, which I did, and when I had read it, my dark heart wrought on this manner, that there was no mercy for me, that the bleffings were gone, and the curfes came in their room, and that I had loft my opportunity. But the Lord helped me ftill to go on reading, till I came to ch. 30. the feven firft verfes; where I found there was mercy promifed a-gain if we would return to him by repentance; and though we were fcattered from one end of the earth to the other, yet the Lord would gather us together, and turn all thofe curfes upon our enemies. I do not defire to live to forget this fcripture, and what comfort it was to me

Now the *Indians* began to talk of removing from this place, fome one way and fome another. There were now befides my felf nine *English* captives in this place (all of them children except one woman) I got an opportunity to go and take my leave of them, they being to go one way and I another. I afked them whether they were earneft with God for deliverance, they told me they did as they were able, and it was fome comfort to me, that the Lord ftirred up children to look to him. The woman, viz. good wife *Joflin* told me fhe fhould never fee me again, and that fhe could find in her heart to ran away by any means, for we were near thirty miles from any *English* town, and fhe very big with child, having but one week to reckon; and another child in her arms two years old, and bad rivers there were to go over, and we were feeble with our poor and courfe entertainment. I had my Bible with me, I pulled it out, and afked her whether fhe would read; we opened the Bible, and lighted on *Pfal.* 27. in which Pfalm we efpecially took notice of that verfe, *Wait on the Lord, be of good courage, and he fhall ftrengthen thine heart, wait I fay on the Lord*

The

The fourth Remove.

AND now muſt I part with the little company I had Here I parted with my daughter *Mary* (whom I never ſaw again till I ſaw her in *Dorcheſter*, returned from captivity) and from four little couſins and neighbours, ſome of which I never ſaw afterward, the Lord only knows the end of them. Among them alſo was that poor woman before mentioned who came to a ſad end, as ſome of the company told me in my travel : She having much grief upon her ſpirits about her miſerable condition, being ſo near her time, ſhe would be often aſking the *Indians* to let her go home : they not being willing to that, and ye vexed with her importunity gathered a great company together about her, and ſtript her naked and ſet her in the midſt of them ; and when they had ſung and danced about her (in their helliſh manner) as long as they pleaſed, they knock'd her on the head, and the child in her arms with her : When they had done that, they made a fire and put them both into it, and told the other children that were with them, that if they attempted to go home, they would ſerve them in like manner. The children ſaid ſhe did not ſhed one tear, but prayed all the while. But to return to my own journey : We travelled about half a day or a little more and came to a deſolate place in the wilderneſs where there were no wigwams or inhabitants before ; we came about the middle of the afternoon to this place ; cold, wet and ſnowy, and hungry, and weary, and no refreſhing for man, but the cold ground to ſit on, and our poor *Indian* cheer.

Heart-aching thoughts here I had about my poor children, who were ſcattered up and down among the wild beaſts of the foreſt : My head was light and diffy (either through hunger or bad lodging, or trouble, or all together) my knees feeble, my body raw by ſetting double night and day, that I cannot expreſs to man, the affliction that lay upon my ſpirit, but the Lord helped me at that time to expreſs it to himſelf. I opened my *Bible* to read, and the Lord brought that precious ſcripture to me, *Jer.* 31. 16. *Thus ſaith the Lord, refrain thy voice from weeping, and thine eyes from tears, for thy work ſhall be rewarded, and they ſhall come again from the land of the enemy.* This was a ſweet cordial to me, when I was ready to faint, many and many a time have I ſat down and wept ſweetly over this ſcripture. At this place we continued about four days.

The fifth Remove.

THE occaſion (as I thought) of their removing at this time, was the *Engliſh* army's being near and following them : For they went as if they had gone for their lives, for ſome conſiderable way ; and then they made a ſtop, and choſe out ſome of their

ſtouteſt

ftouteft men, and fent them back to hold the *Englifh* army in play whilft the reft efcaped ; and then like *Jehu* they marched on furioufly with their old and young: fome carried their old decriped mothers. fome carried one, and fome another. Four of them carried a great *Indian* upon a bier ; but going through a thick wood with him they were hindred, and could make no hafte ; whereupon they took him upon their backs, and carried him one at a time, till we came to *Bacquag* river. Upon *Friday* a little afternoon we came to this river. When all the company was come up and were gathered together, I thought to count the number of them but they were fo many. and being fomewhat in motion, it was beyond my fkill. In this travel, becaufe of my wound, I was fomewhat favoured in my load: I carried only my knitting-work, and two quarts of parched meal : Being very faint, I afked my miftrefs to give me one fpoonful of the meal, but fhe would not give me a tafte. They quickly fell to cutting dry trees, to make rafts to carry them over the river, and foon my turn came to go over. By the advantage of fome brufh which they had laid upon the raft to fit on, I did not wet my foot (while many of themfelves at the other end were mid-leg deep) which cannot but be acknowledged as a favour of God to my weakened body. it being a very cold time. I was not before acquainted with fuch kind of doings or dangers. *When thou paffeft through the waters I will be with thee, and through the rivers they fhall not overflow thee. Ifai. 43. 2.* A certain number of us got over the river that night, but it was the night after the *Sabbath* before all the company was got over. On the *Saturday* they boiled an old horfe's leg (which they had got) and fo we drank of the broth, as foon as they thought it was ready, and when it was almoft all gone, they fill'd it up again. The firft week of my being among them, I hardly eat any thing: the fecond week I found my ftomach grow very faint for want of fomething; and yet it was very hard to get down their filthy trafh ; but the third week (though I could think how formerly my ftomach would turn againft this or that, and I could ftarve and die before I could eat fuch things, yet) they were pleafant and favoury to my tafte. I was at this time knitting a pair of white cotton ftockings for my miftrefs, and I had not yet wrought upon the *Sabbath* day : When the *Sabbath* came, they bid me go to work ; I told them it was *Sabbath* day, and defired them to let me reft, and told them I would do as much more work to-morrow ; to which they anfwered me, they would break my face. And here I cannot but take notice of the ftrange Providence of God in preferving the heathen: They were many hundreds, old and young, fome fick, and fome lame ; many had *Papoofes* at their backs ; the greateft number at this time with us were *Squaws*, and they travelled

with

with all they had, bag and baggage, and yet they got over this
river aforesaid ; and on *Monday* they sat their wigwams on fire,
and away they went ; on that very day came the *English* army after
them to this river, and saw the smoke of their wigwams, and yet
this river put a stop to them. God did not give them courage or
activity to go over after us : We were not ready for so great a
mercy as victory and deliverance ; if we had been, God would have
found out a way for the *English* to have passed this river, as well
as for the *Indians* with their *Squaws* and children, and all their
luggage. *O that my people had hearkened unto me, and Israel had
walked in my ways, I should soon have subdued their enemies, and
turned my hand against their adversaries.* Psal. 81. 13, 14.

The sixth Remove.

ON *Monday* (as I said) they sat their wigwams on fire, and
went away. It was a cold morning, and before us there
was a great brook with ice on it : Some waded through it up to
the knees and higher, but others went till they came to a beaver-dam,
and I amongst them, where, through the good Providence of God,
I did not wet my foot. I went along that day mourning and lamenting (leaving farther my own country and travelling farther
into the vast and howling wilderness) and I understood something
of *Lot*'s wife's temptation, when she looked back : We came that
day to a great swamp, by the side of which we took up our lodging
that night. When we came to the brow of the hill that looked toward the swamp. I thought we had been come to a great *Indian*
town (though there were none but our own company) the *Indians*
were as thick as the trees ; it seemed as if there had been a thou-
sand hatchets going at once : If one looked before one there was
nothing but *Indians*, and behind one nothing but *Indians* ; and so
on either hand ; and I myself in the midst, and no christian soul near
.... and yet how hath the Lord preserved me in safety ! Oh the experience that I have had of the goodness of God to me and mine !

The seventh Remove.

AFTER a restless and hungry night there, we had a wearisome
time of it the next day. The swamp, by which we lay, was
as it were a deep dungeon, and an exceeding high and steep hill
before it. Before I got to the top of the hill, I thought my heart
and legs and all would have broken, and failed me. What through
faintness and soreness of body, it was a grievous day of travel to me.
As we went along, I saw a place where *English* cattle had been,
that was a comfort to me, such as it was : Quickly after that we
came to an *English* path, which so took me, that I thought I could
there

there have freely lien down and died. That day, a little after noon, we came to *Sqauheag*, where the *Indians* quickly spread themselves over the deserted *English* fields, gleaning what they could find; some pick'd up ears of wheat that were crickled down, some found ears of *Indian* corn, some found ground-nuts, and others sheaves of wheat that were frozen together in the shock, and went to threshing of them out. Myself got two ears of *Indian* corn, and whilst I did but turn my back, one of them was stolen from me, which much troubled me. There came an *Indian* to them at that time, with a basket of *horse-liver*; I asked him to give me a piece: What, (says he) can you eat *horse-liver?* I told him I would try, if he would give me a piece, which he did; and I laid it on the coals to roast, but before it was half ready, they got half of it away from me; so that I was forced to take the rest and eat it as it was, with the blood about my mouth, and yet a savory bit it was to me; for to the hungry soul every bitter thing was sweet. A solemn sight methought it was, to see whole fields of wheat and *Indian* corn forsaken and spoiled, and the remainder of them to be food for our mercilefs enemies. That night we had a mefs of wheat for our supper.

The eighth Remove.

ON the morrow morning we must go over *Connecticut* river to meet with King *Philip*; two canoes full they had carried over, the next turn my self was to go; but as my foot was upon the canoe to step in, there was a sudden out-cry among them, and I must step back; and instead of going over the river, I must go four or five miles up the river farther *Northward*. Some of the *Indians* ran one way and some another. The cause of this rout was, as I tho't, their espying some *English* scouts, who were there-abouts. In this travel up the river, about noon the company made a stop, and sat down, some to eat and others to rest them. As I sat amongst them, musing on things past, my son *Joseph* unexpectedly came to me: We asked of each others welfare, bemoaning our doleful condition, and the change that had come upon us: We had husband, and father, and children, and sisters, and friends and relations, and house, and home, and many comforts of this life; but now we might say as *Job, Naked came I out of my mother's womb, and naked shall I return: The Lord gave, and the Lord hath taken away, blessed be the name of the Lord.* I asked him whether he would read? he told me he earnestly desired it. I gave him my Bible, and he lighted upon that comfortable scripture, *Psalm* 118. 17, 18. *I shall not die, but live, and declare the works of the Lord: The Lord hath chastened me sore, yet he hath not given me over to death.* Look

here

here mother, (says he) did you read this? And here I may take occasion to mention one principal ground of my setting forth these lines, even as the Psalmist says, to declare the works of the Lord, and his wonderful power in carrying us along, preserving us in the wilderness, while under the enemy's hand, and returning of us in safety again; and his goodness in bringing to my hand so many comfortable and suitable scriptures in my distress.

But to return: We travelled on till night, and in the morning we must go over the river to *Philip*'s crew. When I was in the canoe, I could not but be amazed at the numerous crew of Pagans that were on the bank on the other side. When I came ashore, they gathered all about me, I sitting alone in the midst: I observed they asked one another questions, and laughed, and rejoiced over their gains and victories. Then my heart began to fail, and I fell a weeping; which was the first time to my remembrance, that I wept before them; although I had met with so much affliction, and my heart was many times ready to break, yet could I not shed one tear in their sight, but rather had been all this while in a maze, and like one astonished; but now I may say as *Psal.* 137. 1. *By the river of Babylon, there we sat down, yea, we wept, when we remembered Zion.* There one of them asked me why I wept? I could hardly tell what to say; yet I answered, they would kill me: No said he, none will hurt you. Then came one of them, and gave me two spoonfuls of meal (to comfort me) and another gave me half a pint of peas which was worth more than many bushels at another time. Then I went to see King *Philip*: he bid me come in, and sit down; and asked me whether I would smoke it? (a usual compliment now a days, among the saints and sinners) but this no ways suited me. For though I had formerly used tobacco, yet I had left it ever since I was first taken. It seems to be a bait the devil lays to make men lose their precious time. I remember with shame how formerly, when I had taken two or three pipes, I was presently ready for another: such a bewitching thing it is: But I thank God, he has now given me power over it; surely there are many who may be better employed, than to sit sucking a stinking tobacco-pipe.

Now the *indians* gathered their forces to go against *Northampton*: Over night one went about yelling and hooting to give notice of the design. Whereupon they went to boiling of groundnuts, and parching corn (as many as had it) for their provision; and in the morning away they went. During my abode in this place, *Philip* spake to me to make a shirt for his boy, which I did; for which he gave me a shilling; I offered the money to my mistress, but she bid me keep it, and with it I bought a piece of
borse

horfe-flefh. Afterward he afked me to make a cap for his boy, for which he invited me to dinner: I went, and he gave me a pan-cake, about as big as two fingers; it was made of parched wheat, beaten, and fried in bear's greafe but I thought I never tafted pleafanter meat in my life There was a *Squaw* who fpake to me to make a fhirt for her *Sannup* ; for which fhe gave me a piece of beef. Another afked me to knit a pair of ftockings, for which fhe gave me a quart of peas. I boiled my peas and beef together, and invited my mafter and miftrefs to dinner ; but the proud goffip, becaufe I ferved them both in one difh, would eat nothing, except one bit that he gave her upon the point of his knife. Hearing that my fon was come to this place, I went to fee him, and found him lying flat on the ground ; I afked him how he could fleep fo ? he anfwered me, that he was not afleep, but at prayer ; and that he lay fo, that they might not obferve what he was doing. I pray God he may remember thefe things now he is returned in fafety. At this place (the fun now getting higher) what with the beams and heat of the fun, and the fmoke of the wigwams, I thought I fhould have been blinded. I could fcarce dif-cern one wigwam from another. There was one *Mary Thurfton* of *Medfield*, who feeing how it was with me, lent me a hat to wear ; but as foon as I was gone, the *Squaw* that owned that *Mary Thurfton*, came running after me, and got it away again. Here was a *Squaw* who gave me a fpoonful of meal, I put it in my pocket to keep it fafe, yet notwithftanding fome body ftole it. but put five *Indian* corns in the room of it ; which corns were the greateft provifion I had in my travel for one day.

The *Indians* returning from *North-Hampton*, brought with them fome horfes, and fheep, and other things which they had taken : I defired them that they would carry me to *Albany* upon one of thofe horfes, and fell me for powder ; for fo they had fometimes dif-courfed. I was utterly helplefs of getting home on foot, the way that I came. I could hardly bear to think of the many weary fteps I had taken to this place.

The ninth Remove.

BUT inftead of either going to *Albany* or home-ward, we muft go five miles up the river, and then go over it. Here we abode a while. Here lived a forry *Indian*, who fpake to me to make him a fhirt, when I had done it, he would pay me nothing for it. But he living by the river fide, where I often went to fetch water, I would often be putting him in mind, and calling for my pay ; at laft he told me, if I would make another fhirt for a Pa-poos not yet born, he would give me a knife, which he did, when

I had done it. I carried the knife in, and my master asked me to give it him, and I was not a little glad that I had any thing that they would accept of, and be pleased with. When we were at this place, my master's maid came home : she had been gone three weeks into the *Narraganset* country to fetch corn, where they had stored up some in the ground : She brought home about a peck and a half of corn. This was about the time that their great Captain *(Nannanto)* was killed in the *Narraganset* country.

My son being now about a mile from me, I asked liberty to go and see him, they bid me go and away I went ; but quickly lost myself, travelling over hills and through swamps, and could not find the way to him. And I cannot but admire at the wonderful power and goodness of God to me, in that though I was gone from home and met with all sorts of *Indians*, and those I had no knowledge of, and there being no christian soul near me, yet not one of them offered the least imaginable miscarriage to me. I turned homeward again, and met with my master, and he shewed me the way to my son. When I came to him, I found him not well ; and withal he had a boil on his side, which much troubled him : We bemoaned one another a while as the Lord helped us, and then I returned again. When I was returned, I found myself as unsatisfied as I was before. I went up and down mourning and lamenting, and my spirit was ready to sink, with the thoughts of my poor children : My son was ill, and I could not but think of his mournful looks, having no christian friend near him, to do any office of love to him, either for soul or body. And my poor girl, I knew not where she was, nor whether she was sick or well, alive or dead. I repaired under these thoughts to my Bible, (my great comfort in that time) and that scripture came to my hand, *Cast thy burden upon the Lord, and he shall sustain thee* Psalm 55. 22.

But I was fain to go look after something to satisfy my hunger : And going among the wigwams, I went into one, and there found a Squaw who shewed herself very kind to me, and gave me a piece of bear. I put it into my pocket, and came home ; but could not find an opportunity to broil it, for fear they should get it from me ; and there it lay all the day and night in my stinking pocket. In the morning I went again to the same Squaw, who had a kettle of ground-nuts boiling : I asked her to let me boil my piece of bear in the kettle, which she did, and gave me some ground nuts to eat with it, and I cannot but think how pleasant it was to me. I have sometimes seen bear baked handsomely amongst the *English*, and some liked it, but the thoughts that it was bear, made me tremble : But now that was savory to me that one would think was enough to turn the stomach of a brute-creature,

C

One

One bitter cold day, I could find no room to fit down before the fire: I went out, and could not tell what to do, but I went into another wigwam, where they were also fitting round the fire; but the Squaw laid a fkin for me, and bid me fet down, and gave me fome ground nuts, and bid me come again: and told me they would buy me if they were able; and yet thefe were ftrangers to me that I never knew before.

The tenth Remove.

THAT day a fmall part of the company removed about three quarters of a mile, intending farther the next day. When they came to the place they intended to lodge, and had pitched their wigwams, being hungry, I went again back to the place we were before at, to get fomething to eat; being encouraged by the Squaw's kindnefs, who bid me come again. When I was there, there came an *Indian* to look after me; who when he had found me, kickt me all-along. I went home and found venifon roafting that night, but they would not give me one bit of it. Sometimes I met with favour, and fometimes with nothing but frowns.

The eleventh Remove.

THE next day in the morning, they took their travel, intending a day's journey up the river; I took my load at my back, and quickly we came to wade over a river, and paffed over tirefome and wearifome hills. One hill was fo fteep, that I was fain to creep up upon my knees, and to hold by the twigs and bufhes to keep myfelf from falling backward. My head alfo was fo light that I ufually reeled as I went: But I hope all thofe wearifome fteps that I have taken, are but a forwarding of me to the heavenly reft. *I know, O Lord, that thy judgments are right, and that thou in faithfulnefs hath afflicted me. Pfalm* 119. 75.

The twelfth Remove.

IT was upon a Sabbath day morning, that they prepared for their travel. This morning I afked my mafter whether he would fell me to my hufband? he anfwered *nux*; which did much rejoice my fpirit. My miftrefs, before we went, was gone to the burial of a *Papoos*, and returning. fhe found me fitting, and reading in my Bible: She fnatcht it haftily out of my hand, and threw it out of doors; I ran out and catcht it up, and put it into my pocket, and never let her fee it afterwards. Then they packed up their things to be gone, and gave me my load: I complained it was too heavy, whereupon fhe gave me a flap on the face, and bid me be gone. I lifted up my heart to God, hoping that redemption was not far off; and the rather becaufe their infolence grew worfe and worfe.   But

But thoughts of my going homeward (for fo we bent our courfe) much cheered my fpirit, and made my burden feem light, and almoft nothing at all. But (to my amazement and great perplexity) the fcale was foon turned ; for when we had got a little way. on a fudden my miftrefs gave out, fhe would go no further, but turn back again, and faid I muft go back again with her, and fhe called her Sannup, and would have had him go back alfo, but he wou'd not ; but faid, he would go on, and come to us again in three days. My fpirit was upon this (I confefs) very impatient, and almoft outrageous. I thought I could as well have died as went back. I cannot declare the trouble that I was in about it ; back again I muft go. As foon as I had an opportunity, I took my Bible to read, and that quieting fcripture came to my hand, *Pfalm* 46. 10. *Be ftill and know that I am God.* Which ftilled my fpirit for the prefent : but a fore time of trial I concluded I had to go through. My mafter being gone, who feemed to me the beft friend I had of an *Indian*, both in cold and hunger, and quickly fo it proved Down I fat with my heart as full as it could hold, and yet fo hungry, that I could not fit neither : But going out to fee what I could find, and walking among the trees, I found fix acorns and two chefnuts, which were fome refrefhment to me. Towards night I gathered me fome fticks for my own comfort, that I might not lie a cold ; but when we came to lie down, they bid me go out, and lie fomewhere elfe, for they had company (they faid come in more than their own :) I told them I could not tell where to go, they bid me go look : I told them, if I went to another wigwam they would be angry, and fend me home again. Then one of the company drew his fword, and told me he would run me through if I did not go prefently. Then was I fain to ftoop to this rude fellow, and go out in the night, I knew not whither. Mine eyes hath feen that fellow afterwards walking up and down in *Bofton*, under the appearance of a friendly *Indian*, and feveral others of the like cut. I went to one wigwam, and they told me they had no room. Then I went to another, and they faid the fame : At laft an old *Indian* bid me come to him, and his Squaw gave me fome ground-nuts; fhe gave me alfo fomething to lay under my head, and a good fire we had : Through the good providence of God, I had a comfortable lodging that night. In the morning another *Indian* bid me come at night and he would give me fix ground-nuts, which I did. We were at this place and time about two miles from *Connecticut* river. We went in the morning (to gather ground-nuts) to the river, and went back again at night. I went with a great load at my back (for they when they went, tho' but a little way would carry all their trumpery with them) I told them the fkin was off my back, but I had no other comforting anfwer from them than this, that it would be no matter if my head was off too.

The

The thirteenth Remove.

INSTEAD of going towards the *Bay* (which was what I defired) I muſt go with them five or ſix miles down the river, into
a mighty thicket of bruſh, where we abode almoſt a fortnight.
Here one aſked me to make a ſhirt for her papoos for which ſhe gave
me a meſs of broth, which was thickned with meal made of the bark
of a tree; and to make it better ſhe had put into it about a handful
of peas, and a few roaſted ground-nuts. I had not ſeen my ſon a
pretty while, and here was an *Indian* of whom I made enquiry after him, and aſked him when he ſaw him? He anſwered me,
that ſuch a time his maſter roaſted him, and that himſelf did eat a
piece of him as big as his two fingers, and that he was very good
meat. But the Lord upheld my ſpirit under this Diſcouragement;
and I conſidered their horrible addictedneſs to lying, and that
there is not one of them that makes the leaſt conſcience of ſpeaking the truth.

In this place, one cold night, as I lay by the fire, I removed a
ſtick which kept the heat from me, a Squaw moved it down again,
at which I looked up, and ſhe threw an handful of aſhes in my
eyes; I thought I ſhould have been quite blinded and never have
ſeen more: But lying down, the water ran out of my eyes, and
carried the dirt with it, that by the morning I recovered my ſight
again. Yet upon this, and the like occaſions, I hope it is not too
much to ſay with *Job, Have pity upon me, have pity upon me. O
ye my friends, for the hand of the LORD has touched me.* And
here I cannot but remember how many times ſitting in their wigwams, and muſing on things paſt, I ſhould ſuddenly leap up and
run out, as if I had been at home, forgetting where I was, and
what my condition was, but when I was without, and ſaw nothing
but wilderneſs and woods, and a company of barbarous Heathen,
my mind quickly returned to me, which made me think of that
ſpoken concerning *Samſon*, who ſaid *I will go out and ſhake
myſelf as at other times, but he wiſt not that the Lord was departed from him.*

About this time, I began to think that all my hopes of reſtora-
tion would come to nothing. I thought of the *Engliſh* army, and
hoped for their coming, and being retaken by them, but that failed.
I hoped to be carried to *Albany*, as the *Indians* had diſcourſed, but
that failed alſo.

I thought of being ſold to my huſband, as my maſter ſpake; but
inſtead of that, my maſter himſelf was gone, and I left behind, ſo
that my ſpirit was now quite ready to ſink. I aſked them to let
me go out and pick up ſome ſticks, that I might get alone, and
pour out my heart unto the Lord. Then alſo I took my Bible to
read,

read, but I found no comfort here neither, yet I can say, in all my sorrows and afflictions, God did not leave me to have any impatient work toward himself, as if his ways were unrighteous; but I knew that he laid upon me less than I deserved. Afterward, before this doleful time ended with me, I was turning the leaves of my Bible, and the Lord brought to me some scripture which did a little revive me, as that, *Isa.* 55. 8. *For my thoughts are not your thoughts, neither are my ways your ways, saith the Lord.* And also that, *Psalm* 37. 5. *Commit thy ways unto the Lord, trust also in him, and he shall bring it to pass.*

About this time they came yelping from *Hadley*, having there killed three *Englishmen*, and brought one captive with them, *viz. Thomas Read.* They all gathered about the poor man, asking him many questions. I desired also to go and see him; and when I came he was crying bitterly, supposing they would quickly kill him. Whereupon I asked one of them, whether they intended to kill him, he answered me, they would not.: He being a little cheered with that, I asked him about the welfare of my husband, he told me he saw him such a time in the *Bay*, and he was well, but very melancholy. By which I certainly understood (though I suspected it before) that whatsoever the *Indians* told me respecting him, was vanity and lies. Some of them told me he was dead, and they had killed him: Some said he was married again, and that the governor wished him to marry, and told him that he should have his choice, and that all persuaded him I was dead. So like were these barbarous creatures to him who was a liar from the beginning.

As I was sitting once in the wigwam here, *Philip's* maid came with the child in her arms, and asked me to give her a piece off my apron, to make a flap for it; I told her I would not; then my mistress bid me give it, but I still said no. The maid told me, if I would not give her a piece, she would tear a piece off it: I told her I would tear her coat then: With that my mistress rises up, and takes up a stick big enough to have killed me, and struck at me with it, but I stept out, and she struck the stick into the mat of the wigwam. But while she was pulling it out, I ran to the maid, and gave her all my apron; and so that storm went over.

Hearing that my son was come to this place, I went to see him, and told him his father was well, but very melancholy: He told me he was as much grieved for his father as for himself: I wondered at his speech, for I thought I had enough upon my spirit, in reference to myself, to make me mindless of my husband, and every one else, they being safe among their friends. He told me also, that a while before, his master (together with other *Indians*) were going to the *French* for powder, but by the way the *Mohawks* met

with

with them, and killed four of their company, which made the rest turn back again ; for which I defire that myfelf and he may ever blefs the Lord; for it might have been worfe with him, had be been fold to the *French*, than it proved to be in his remaining with the *Indians*.

I went to fee an *Englifh* youth in this place, one *John Gilbert*, of *Springfield*. I found him lying without doors upon the ground ; I afked him how he did ; he told me he was very fick of a flux with eating fo much blood. They had turned him out of the wig-wam, and with him an *Indian* Papoos, almoft dead, whofe parents had been killed, in a bitter cold day, without fire or cloaths : The young man himfelf had nothing on but his fhirt and waiftcoat.—— This fight was enough to melt a heart of flint.——There they lay quivering in the cold, the youth round like a dog, the Papoos ftretched out, with his eyes, nofe, and mouth full of dirt, and yet alive, and groaning. I advifed *John* to go and get to fome fire ; he told me he could not ftand, but I perfuaded him ftill, left he fhould lie there and die. And with much ado I got him to a fire, and went myfelf home. As foon as I was got home, his mafter's daughter came after me, to know what I had done with the *Eng-lifhman* ? I told her I had got him to a fire in fuch a place. Now had I need to pray *Paul*'s prayer, 2 *Theff*. 3. 2. *That we may be delivered from unreafonable and wicked men.* For her fatisfaction I went along with her, and brought her to him ; but before I got home again, it was noifed about, that I was running away, and getting the *Englifh* youth along with me : That as foon as I came in, they began to rant and domineer, afking me where I had been, and what I had been doing ? and faying they would knock me on the head : I told them I had been feeing the *Englifh* youth, and that I would not run away. They told me I lied, and getting up a hatchet, they came to me, and faid they would knock me down if I ftirred out again ; and fo confined me to the wigwam. Now may I fay with *David*, 1 *Sam*. 24. 14. *I am in a great ftrait.* If I keep in, I muft die with hunger ; and if I go out, I muft be knocked on the head. This diftreffed condition held that day, and half the next ; and then the Lord remembered me, whofe mer-cies are great. Then came an *Indian* to me with a pair of ftock-ings which were too big for him, and he would have me ravel them out, and knit them fit for him. I fhewed myfelf willing, and bid him afk my miftrefs if I might go along with him a little way ? She faid, yes, I might ; but I was not a little refrefhed with that news, that I had my liberty again. Then I went along with him, and he gave me fome roafted ground-nuts, which did again revive my feeble ftomach.

Being got out of her fight, I had time and liberty again to look into my Bible, which was my guide by day, and my pillow by night. Now that comfortable fcripture prefented itfelf to me, *Ifa.* 45. 7. *For a fmall moment have I forfaken thee, but with great mercies will I gather thee.* Thus the Lord carried me along from one time to another, and made good to me this precious promife, and many others   Then my fon came to fee me, and I afked his mafter to let him ftay a while with me, that I might comb his head, and look over him, for he was almoft overcome with lice.   He told me when I had done, that he was very hungry, but I had nothing to relieve him, but bid him go into the wigwams as he went along, and fee if he could get any thing among them. Which he did, and (it feems) tarried a little too long, for his mafter was angry with him, and beat him, and then fold him.   Then he came running to tell me he had a new mafter, and that he had given him fome ground-nuts already.   Then I went along with him to his new mafter, who told me he loved him, and he fhould not want.   So his mafter carried him away, and I never faw him afterward, till I faw him at *Pifcataqua* in *Portfmouth*.

That night they bid me go out of the wigwam again : My miftrefs's Papoos was fick, and it died that night ; and there was one benefit in it, that there was more room.   I went to a wigwam, and they bid me come in, and gave me a fkin to lie upon, and a mefs of venifon and ground-nuts, which was a choice difh among them. On the morrow they buried the Papoos ; and afterward, both morning and evening, there came a company to mourn and howl with her : Though I confefs I could not much condole with them. Many forrowful days I had in this place ; often getting alone, *like a crane or a fwallow, fo did I chatter ; I did mourn as a dove, mine eyes fail with looking upward.   O Lord I am oppreffed, undertake for me*   *Ifai.* 38. 14.   I could tell the Lord as *Hezekiah, Ver.* 3. *Remember now O Lord, I befeech thee, how I have walked before thee in truth.*   Now had I time to examine all my ways : My confcience did not accufe me of unrighteoufnefs towards one or another ; yet I faw how in my walk with God, I had been a carelefs creature.   As *David* faid, *againft thee only have I finned.*   And I might fay with the poor publican, *God be merciful unto me a finner*.   Upon the Sabbath days I could look upon the fun, and think how people were going to the houfe of God to have their fouls refrefh'd, and then home and their bodies alfo ; but I was deftitute of both, and might fay as the poor prodigal, *He would fain have filled his belly with the hufks that the fwine did eat, and no man gave unto him.   Luke* 15. 16.   For I muft fay with him, *Father I have finned againft heaven and in thy fight.*   Ver. 21.   I remember how on the night before and after the

the Sabbath, when my family was about me, and relations and neighbours with us ; we could pray, and fing, and refresh our bodies with the good creatures of God, and then have a comfortable bed to lie down on ; but instead of all this, I had only a little swill for the body, and then like a swine, must lie down on the ground. I cannot express to man, the sorrow that lay upon my spirit, the Lord knows it. Yet that comfortable scripture would often come to my mind, *For a small moment have I forsaken thee, but with great mercies will I gather thee.*

The fourteenth Remove.

NOW must we pack up and be gone from this thicket, bending our course toward the bay-towns. I having nothing to eat by the way this day, but a few crumbs of cake. that an *Indian* gave my girl, the same day we were taken. She gave it me, and I put it into my pocket : There it lay, till it was so mouldy (for want of good baking) that one could not tell what it was made of ; it fell all into crumbs, and grew so dry and hard, that it was like little flints ; and this refreshed me many times, when I was ready to faint. It was in my thoughts when I put it to my mouth, that if ever I returned, I would tell the world, what a blessing the Lord gave to such mean food. As we went along, they killed a deer, with a young one in her ; they gave me a piece of the fawn, and it was so young and tender, that one might eat the bones as well as the flesh, and yet I thought it very good. When night came on, we sat down ; it rained, but they quickly got up a bark wigwam, where I lay dry that night. I looked out in the morning, and many of them had lien in the rain all night, I saw by their reaking. Thus the Lord dealt mercifully with me many times, and I fared better than many of them. In the morning they took the blood of the deer, and put it into the paunch, and so boiled it : I could eat nothing of that, though they eat it sweetly. And yet they were so nice in other things, that when I had fetch'd water, and had put the dish I dip'd the water with into the kettle of water which I brought, they would say they would knock me down, for they said it was a sluttish trick.

The fifteenth Remove.

WE went on our travel. I having got an handful of ground nuts for my support that day : They gave me my load, and I went on cheerfully (with the thoughts of going homeward) having my burthen more upon my back than my spirit. We came to Baquaug river again that day, near which we abode a few days. Sometimes one of them would give me a pipe, another a little tobacco, another a little salt, which I would change for victuals I

cannot

cannot but think what a wolvish appetite persons have in a starving condition; for many times, when they gave me that which was hot, I was so greedy, that I should burn my mouth, that it would trouble me many hours after, and yet I should quickly do the like again. And after I was thoroughly hungry, I was never again satisfied. For though it sometimes fell out that I had got enough, and did eat till I could eat no more; yet I was as unsatisfied as I was when I began. And now could I see that scripture verified, there being many scriptures that we do not take notice of, or understand till we are afflicted, *Mic. 6. 14. Thou shalt eat and not be satisfied* Now might I see more than ever before, the miseries that sin hath brought upon us. Many times I should be ready to run out against the heathen, but that scripture would quiet me again, *Amos 3. 6. Shall there be evil in the city, and the Lord hath not done it?* The Lord help me to make a right improvement of his word, and that I might learn that great lesson, *Mic. 6. 8. 9. He hath shewed thee, O man, what is good, and what doth the Lord require of thee, but to do justly, and love mercy, and walk humbly with thy God? Hear ye the rod, and who hath appointed it.*

The sixteenth Remove.

WE began this remove with wading over *Baquaug* river. The water was up to our knees, and the stream very swift, and so cold, that I thought it would have cut me in sunder. I was so week and feeble, that I reeled as I went along, and thought there I must end my days at last, after my bearing and getting through so many difficulties. The *Indians* stood laughing to see me staggering along, but in my distress, the Lord gave me experience of the truth and goodness of that promise, *Isa 43. 2. When thou passest through the waters I will be with thee, and through the rivers, they shall not overflow thee.* Then I sat down to put on my stockings and shoes, with the tears running down my eyes, and many sorrowful thoughts in my heart. But I got up to go along with them. Quickly there came up to us an *Indian* who informed them, that I must go to *Wachuset* to my master for there was a letter come from the council to the *Saggamores* about redeeming the captives, and that there would be another in 4 days, and that I must be there ready. My heart was so heavy before, that I could scarce speak, or go in the path; and yet now so light that I could run. My strength seemed to come again, and to recruit my feeble knees, and aching heart; yet it pleased them to go but one mile that night, and there we stayed two days. In that time came a company of *Indians* to us, near thirty, all on horse-back. My heart skipt within me, thinking they had been *Englishmen*, at the first sight of them: For they were dressed in *English* apparel,
D
with

with hats, white neckcloths, and fashes about their waifts, and ribbons upon their fhoulders : But when they came near, there was a vaft difference between the lovely faces of chriftians, and the foul looks of thofe heathen, which much damped my fpirits again.

The feventeenth Remove.

A Comfortable remove it was to me, becaufe of my hopes. They gave me my pack and along we went cheerfully ; but quickly my will proved more than my ftrength ; having little or no refrefhment, my ftrength failed, and my fpirits were almoft quite gone. Now may I fay as *David, Pfalm* 109. 22. 23. 24. *I am poor and needy, and my heart is wounded within me. I am gone like the fhadow when it declineth : I am toffed up and down like the locuft : My knees are weak through fafting, and my flefh faileth of fatnefs.* At right we came to an *Indian* town, and the *Indians* fat down by a wigwam difcourfing, but I was almoft fpent and could fcarce fpeak. I laid down my load, and went into the wigwam, and there fat an *Indian* boiling of horfe-feet (they being wont to eat the flefh firft, and when the feet were old and dried, and they had nothing elfe, they would cut off the feet and ufe them) I afked him to give me a little of his broth, or water they were boiling in : He took a difh, and gave me one fpoonful of famp, and bid me take as much of the broth as I would. Then I put fome of the hot water to the famp, and drank it up, and my fpirits came again. He gave me alfo a piece of the ruffe, or ridding of the fmall guts, and I broiled it on the coals, and now I may fay with *Jonathan, fee I pray you, how mine eyes are enlightened becaufe I tafted a little of this honey.* 1 Sam. 14. 20. Now is my fpirit revived again ; though means be never fo inconfiderable, yet if the Lord beftow his blefling upon them, they fhall refrefh both foul and body.

The eighteenth Remove.

W E took up our packs, and along we went. But a wearifome day I had of it. As we went along, I faw an *Englifhman* ftripped naked, and lying dead upon the ground, but knew not who he was. Then we came to another *Indian* town, where we ftayed all night. In this town there were four *Englifh* children captives, and one of them my own fifter's. I went to fee how fhe did, and fhe was well, confidering her captive condition. I would have tarried that night with her, but they that owned her would not fuffer it. Then I went to another wigwam, where they were boiling corn and beans, which was a lovely
fight

fight to fee, but I could not get a tafte thereof. Then I went into another wigwam, where there were two of the *Englifh* children : The Squaw was boiling horfes feet, fhe cut me off a little piece, and gave one of the *Englifh* children a piece alfo. Being very hungry ; I had quickly eat up mine ; but the child could not bite it, it was fo tough and finewy, but lay fucking, gnawing and flabbering of it in the mouth and hand, then I took it of the child, and eat it my felf, and favory it was to my tafte. That I may fay as *Job, Chap.* 6. 7. *The things that my foul refufeth to touch, are as my forrowful meat.* Thus the Lord made that pleafant and refrefhing, which another time would have been an abomination. Then I went home to my miftrefs's wigwam, and they told me I difgraced my mafter with begging, and if I did fo any more, they would knock me on the head : I told them, they had as good do that, as ftarve me to death.

The nineteenth Remove.

THEY faid when we went out, that we muft travel to *Wachufet* this day. But a bitter weary day I had of it, travelling now three days together, without refting any day between. At laft, after many weary fteps, I faw *Wachufet* hills, but many miles off. Then we came to a great fwamp, through which we travelled up to our knees in mud and water, which was heavy going to one tired before. Being almoft fpent, I thought I fhould have funk down at laft, and never got out ; but I may fay as in *Pfalm* 94. 18. *When my foot flipped, thy mercy, O Lord, held me up.*— Going along, having indeed my life, but little fpirit, *Philip* (who was in the company) came up, and took me by the hand, and faid, *Two weeks more and you fhall be miftrefs again.* I afked him if he fpake true ? he anfwered yes, and quickly you fhall come to your mafter again, who had been gone from us three weeks. After many weary fteps, we came to *Wachufet*, where he was, and glad was I to fee him. He afked me when I wafhed me ? I told him not this month ; then he fetched me fome water himfelf, and bid me wafh, and gave me a glafs to fee how I look'd, and bid his Squaw give me fomething to eat. So fhe gave me a mefs of beans and meat, and a little ground-nut cake. I was wonderfully revived with this favour fhewed me. *Pfalm* 106. 46. *He made them alfo to be pitied of all thofe that carried them away captive.*

My mafter had three Squaws, living fometimes with one, and fometimes with another. Onux, this old Squaw at whofe wigwam I was, and with whom my mafter had been thefe three weeks: Another was Wettimore, with whom I had lived and ferved all this while. A fevere and proud dame fhe was ; beftowing every day in dreffing herfelf near as much time as any of the gentry of the

land :

land : Powdering her hair, and painting her face, going with her necklaces, with jewels in her ears, and bracelets upon her hands When she had dressed herself, her work was to make girdles of wampum and beads.   The third Squaw was a younger one. by whom he had two Papooses.   By that time I was refreshed by the old Squaw, Wettimore's maid came to call me home, at which I fell a weeping.   Then the old Squaw told me to encourage me, that when I wanted victuals, I should come to her. and that I should lie in her wigwam.   Then I went with the maid, and quickly I came back and lodged there.   The Squaw laid a mat under me, and a good rug over me ; the first time that I had any such kindness shewed me.   I understood that Wettimore thought, that if she should let me go and serve with the old Squaw, she should be in danger to lose (not only my Service) but the redemption-pay also.   And I was not a little glad to hear this ; being by it raised in my hopes. that in God's due time there would be an end of this sorrowful hour   Then came an *Indian* and asked me to knit him three pair of stockings, for which I had a hat and a silk handkerchief.   Then another asked me to make her a shift, for which she gave me an apron.

Then came *Tom* and *Peter* with the second letter from the council, about the captives.   Though they were *Indians*, I got them by the hand, and burst out into tears ; my heart was so full that I could not speak to them ; but recovering my self, I asked them how my husband did ? and all my friends and acquaintance ? they said they were well. but very melancholy.   They brought me two biskets, and a pound of tobacco. the tobacco I soon gave away : When it was all gone, one asked me to give him a pipe of tobacco, I told him it was all gone ; then he began to rant and threaten ; I told him when my husband came, I would give him some : Hang him rogue, says he, I will knock out his brains, if he comes here   And then again at the same breath, they would say. that if there should come an hundred without guns they would do them no hurt   So unstable and like mad-men they were. So that, fearing the worst, I durst not send to my husband, though there were some thoughts of his coming to redeem and fetch me, not knowing what might follow : for there was but little more trust to them than to the master they served.   When the letter was come the Sagamores met to consult about the captives, and called me to them to enquire how much my husband would give to redeem me.   When I came I sat down among them, as I was wont to do, as their manner is : Then they bid me stand up, and said, they were the general court.   They bid me speak what I thought he would give.   Now knowing that all that we had was destroyed

by

by the *Indians*, I was in a great ſtrait. I thought if I ſhould ſpeak of but a little, it would be ſlighted, and hinder the matter; if of a great ſum, I knew not where it would be procured; yet at a venture, I ſaid twenty pounds, yet deſired them to take leſs; but they would not hear of that, but ſent that meſſage to *Boſton*, that for twenty pounds I ſhould be redeemed. It was a praying *Indian* that wrote their letters for them. There was another praying *Indian*, who told me that he had a brother, that would not eat horſe, his conſcience was ſo tender and ſcrupulous, though as large as hell, for the deſtruction of poor chriſtians, then he ſaid, he read that ſcripture to him, 2 *Kings* 6. 25. *There was a famine in Samaria, and behold they beſieged it, until an aſs's head was ſold for fourſcore pieces of ſilver, and the fourth part of a kab of doves dung, for five pieces of ſilver.* He expounded this place to his brother, and ſhewed him that it was lawful to eat that in a famine, which it is not at another time. And now ſays he, he will eat horſe with any *Indian* of them all. There was another praying *Indian*, who when he had done all the miſchief that he could, betrayed his own father into the *Engliſh*'s hands, thereby to purchaſe his own life. Another praying *Indian* was at *Sudbury* fight, though as he deſerved, he was afterwards hanged for it. There was another praying *Indian*, ſo wicked and cruel, as to wear a ſtring about his neck, ſtrung with chriſtian fingers. Another praying *Indian*, when they went to *Sudbury* fight, went with them, and his Squaw alſo with him, with her papoos at her back: Before they went to that fight, they got a company together to powow : The manner was as followeth.

There was one that kneeled upon a deer-ſkin, with the company round him in a ring, who kneeled, ſtriking upon the ground with their hands, and with ſticks, and muttering or humming with their mouths. Beſides him who kneeled in the ring, there alſo ſtood one with a gun in his hand : Then he on the deer-ſkin made a ſpeech, and all manifeſted aſſent to it, and ſo they did many times together. Then they bid him with a gun go out of the ring, which he did ; but when he was out, they called him in again; but he ſeemed to make a ſtand : Then they called the more earneſtly, till he turned again. Then they all ſang. Then they gave him two guns, in each hand one. And ſo he on the deer-ſkin began again ; and at the end of every ſentence in his ſpeaking, they all aſſented, and humming or muttering with their mouths, and ſtriking upon the ground with their hands. Then they bid him with the two guns, go out of the ring again : which he did a little way. Then they called him again, but he made a ſtand, ſo they called him with greater earneſtneſs :

But

But he stood reeling and wavering, as if he knew not whether he should stand or fall, or which way to go. Then they called him with exceeding great vehemency, all of them, one and another. After a little while he turned in staggering as he went, with his arms stretched out, in each hand a gun. As soon as he came in, they all sang and rejoiced exceedingly a while, and then he upon the deer-skin made another speech, unto which they all assented in a rejoicing manner; and so they ended their business, and forthwith went to *Sudbury* fight.

To my thinking, they went without any scruple but that they should prosper, and gain the victory. And they went out not so rejoicing, but they came home with as great a victory. For they said they killed two captains, and almost an hundred men. One *Englishman* they brought alive with them, and he said it was too true, for they had made sad work at *Sudbury*; as indeed it proved. Yet they came home without that rejoicing and triumphing over their victory, which they were wont to shew at other times : But rather like dogs (as they say) which have lost their ears. Yet I could not perceive that it was for their own loss of men; they said they lost not above five or six ; and I missed none, except in one wigwam. When they went, they acted as if the devil had told them that they should gain the victory, and now they acted as if the devil had told them they should have a fall. Whether it were so or no, I cannot tell, but so it proved : For they quickly began to fall, and so held on that summer, till they came to utter ruin. They came home on a sabbath day, and the pawaw that kneeled upon the deer-skin, came home I may say without any abuse as black as the devil. When my master came home, he came to me and bid me make a shirt for his Papoos, of a holland laced pillowbeer. About that time there came an *Indian* to me, and bid me come to his wigwam at night, and he would give me some pork and ground-nuts. Which I did, and as I was eating, another *Indian* said to me, he seems to be your good friend, but he killed two *Englishmen* at *Sudbury*, and there lie the cloathes behind you ; I looked behind me, and there I saw bloody cloathes, with bullet-holes in them ; yet the Lord suffered not this wretch to do me any hurt, yea instead of that, he many times refresh'd me : Five or six times did he and his Squaw refresh my feeble carcase. If I went to their wigwam at any time, they would always give me something, and yet they were strangers that I never saw before. Another Squaw gave me a piece of fresh pork, and a little salt with it, and lent me her frying-pan to fry it ; and I cannot but remember what a sweet, pleasant and delightful relish that bit had to me, to this day. So little do we prize common mercies, when we have them to the full.

The

The twentieth Remove.

IT was their ufual manner to remove, when they had done any mifchief, left they fhould be found out ; and fo they did at this time. We went about three or four miles, and there they built a great wigwam, big enough to hold an hundred *Indians*, which they did in preparation to a great day of dancing. They would now fay among themfelves, that the governor would be fo angry for his lofs at *Sudbury*, that he would fend no more about the captives, which made me grieve and tremble. My fifter being not far from this place, and hearing that I was here, defired her mafter to let her come and fee me, and he was willing to it, and would come with her ; but fhe being ready firft, told him fhe would go before, and was come within a mile or two of the place : Then he overtook her, and began to rant as if he had been mad, and made her go back again in the rain : So that I never faw her till I faw her in *Charleftown*, but the Lord requited many of their ill doings, for this *Indian* her mafter, was hanged afterwards at *Bofton*. They began now to come from all quarters, againft their merry dancing day : Amongft fome of them came one good-wife *Kettle* : I told her my heart was fo heavy that it was ready to break : So is mine too, faid fhe, but yet I hope we fhall hear fome good news fhortly. I could hear how earneftly my fifter defired to fee me, and I earneftly defired to fee her ; yet neither of us could get an opportunity. My daughter was now but a mile off ; and I had not feen her for nine or ten weeks, as I had not feen my fifter fince our firft taking. I defired them to let me go and fee them, yea I entreated, begged and perfuaded them to let me fee my daughter ; and yet fo hard hearted were they, that they would not fuffer it. They made ufe of their tyrannical power whilft they had it, but through the Lord's wonderful mercy, their time was now but fhort.

On a Sabbath-day, the fun being about an hour high in the afternoon, came Mr. *John Hoar* (the council permitting him, and his own forward fpirit inclining him) together with the two forementioned *Indians*, *Tom* and *Peter*, with the third letter from the council. When they came near, I was abroad ; they prefently called me in, and bid me fit down, and not ftir. Then they catched up their guns and away they ran, as if an enemy had been at hand, and the guns went off apace. I manifefted fome great trouble, and afked them what was the matter ? I told them I thought they had killed the *Englifhman* (for they had in the mean time told me that an *Englifhman* was come) they faid no ; they fhot over his horfe, and under, and before his horfe, and they pufhed him this way and that way, at their pleafure, fhewing what they

they could do. Then they let him come to their wigwams. I begged of them to let me fee the *Englishman*, but they would not ; but there was I fain to fit their pleasure. When they had talked their fill with him, they suffered me to go to him. We asked each other of our welfare, and how my husband did and all my friends ? He told me they were all well, and would be glad to fee me. A-mong other things which my husband sent me, there came a pound of *tobacco*, which I sold for nine shillings in money : For many of them for want of *tobacco*, smoaked *hemlock* and *ground-ivy*. It was a great mistake in any who thought I sent for *tobacco*, for through the favour of God, that desire was overcome. I now asked them whether I should go home with Mr. *Hoar ?* They answered no, one and another of them, and it being late, we lay down with that answer ; in the morning Mr *Hoar* invited the *Saggamores* to dinner ; but when we went to get it ready, we found they had stolen the greatest part of the provision Mr. *Hoar* had brought. And we may fee the wonderful power of God, in that one passage, in that when there was such a number of them together, and so greedy of a little good food, and no *English* there but Mr. *Hoar* and myself, that there they did not knock us on the head, and take what we had ; there being not only some provision, but also trad-ing cloth, a part of the 20 pounds agreed upon : But instead of doing us any mischief, they seemed to be ashamed of the fact, and said it was the *Matchit Indians* that did it. Oh that we could believe that there was nothing too hard for God. God shewed his power over the heathen in this, as he did over the hungry *lions*, when *Daniel* was cast into the *den*. Mr. *Hoar* called them be-time to dinner, but they eat but little, they being so busy in dressing themselves and getting ready for their dance ; which was carried on by eight of them, four men and four Squaws ; my master and mis-tress being two. He was dressed in his holland shirt, with great stockings, his garters hung round with *shillings*, and had girdles of *wampom* upon his head and shoulders. She had a kersey coat, covered with girdles of *wampom* from the loins upward. Her arms from her elbows to her hands, were covered with brace-lets, there were handfuls of necklaces about her neck, and seve-ral sorts of jewels in her ears. She had fine red stockings, and white shoes, her hair powdered, and her face painted red, that was always before black. And all the dancers were after the same manner. There were two others singing and knocking on a kettle for their musick. They kept hopping up and down one after ano-ther, with a kettle of water in the midst, standing warm upon some *embers*, to drink of when they were dry. They held on till almost night, throwing out *wampom* to the standers-by. At night

I

I asked them again, if I should go home? they all as one said no, except my husband would come for me. When we were laid down, my master went out of the wigwam, and by and by sent in an *Indian* called *James the printer*, who told Mr. *Hoar*, that my master would let me go home to-morrow, if he would let him have one pint of liquor. Then Mr. *Hoar* called his own *Indians*, *Tom and Peter*, and bid them all go and see if he would promise it before them three; and if he would he should have it, which he did and had it. *Philip* smelling the business, called me to him, and asked me what I would give him, to tell me some good news, and to speak a good word for me, that I might go home to-morrow i I told him I could not tell what to give him, I would any thing I had, and asked him what he would have? He said two coats, and 20 *shillings* in money, half a bushel of seed corn, and some tobacco. I thanked him for his love, but I knew that good news as well as that crafty fox. My master after he had his drink, quickly came ranting into the *wigwam* again, and called for Mr. *Hoar*, drinking to him and saying he was a good man, and then again he would say, hang him a rogue. Being almost drunk, he would drink to him, and yet presently say he should be hanged: Then he called for me; I trembled to hear him, and yet I was fain to go to him; and he drank to me, shewing no incivility. He was the first *Indian* I saw drunk, all the time I was among them. At last his Squaw ran out, and he after her, round the wigwam, with his money jingling at his knees, but she escaped him; but having an old Squaw, he ran to her, and so through the Lord's mercy, we were no more troubled with him that night. Yet I had not a comfortable night's rest; for I think I can say I did not sleep for three nights together. The night before the letter came from the council, I could not rest, I was so full of fears and troubles; yea, at this time I could not rest night nor day. The next night I was over-joyed, Mr. *Hoar* being come, and that with such good tidings. The third night I was even swallowed up with the thoughts of going home again: and that I must leave my children behind me in the wilderness; so that sleep was now almost departed from mine eyes.

On Tuesday morning they called their *General Court* (as they stiled it) to consult and determine whether I should go home or no. And they all seemingly consented that I should go, except *Philip*, who would not come among them.

But before I go any farther, I would take leave to mention a few remarkable passages of Providence, which I took special notice of in my afflicted time.

1. Of the fair opportunity lost in the long march, a little after the fort fight, when our *English* army was so numerous, and in

E

pursuit

pursuit of the enemy, and so near as to overtake several and destroy them; and the enemy in such distress for food, that our men might track them by their rooting the ground for ground-nuts, whilst they were flying for their lives: I say, that then our army should want provisions, and be obliged to leave their pursuit, and return homeward, and the very next week the enemy came upon our town, like bears bereft of their whelps, or so many ravenous wolves, rending us and our lambs to death, But what shall I say? God seemed to leave his people to themselves, and ordered all things for his own holy ends. *Shall there be evil in the city and the Lord hath not done it? They are not grieved for the affliction of Joseph, therefore they shall go captive, with the first that go captive. It is the Lord's doing, and it should be marvellous in our eyes.*

2. I cannot but remember, how the *Indians* derided the slowness and the dulness of the *English* army in it's setting out. For after the desolations at *Lancaster* and *Medfield,* as I went along with them, they asked me when I thought the *English* army would come after them? I told them I could not tell. It may be they will come in *May,* said they; thus they did scoff at us, as if the *English* would be a quarter of a year getting ready.

3. Which also I have hinted before, when the *English* army with new supplies were sent forth to pursue after the enemy, and they understanding it, fled before them till they came to *Baquaug* river, where they forthwith went over safely; that the river should be impassable to the *English*. I cannot but admire to see the wonderful providence of God, in preserving the Heathen for further affliction to our poor country They could go in great numbers over, but the *English* must stop: God had an over-ruling hand in all those things.

4. It was thought, if their corn were cut down, they would starve and die with hunger; and all that could be found was destroyed, and they driven from that little they had in store, into the woods, in the midst of winter; and yet how to admiration did the Lord preserve them for his holy ends, and the destruction of many still among the *English*! Strangely did the Lord provide for them, that I did not see (all the time I was among them) one man, woman or child die with hunger. Though many times they would eat, that, that a hog or a dog would hardly touch.; yet by that God strengthened them to be a scourge to his people.

Their chief and commonest food was ground nuts, they eat also nuts and acorns, artichokes, lilly roots, ground beans, and several other weeds and roots that I know not.

They would pick up old bones, and cut them in pieces at the joints, and if they were full of worms and maggots, they would scald them over the fire, to make the vermine come out, and then boil

boil them, and drink up the liquor, and then beat the great ends of them in a mortar, and so eat them. They would eat horses guts, and ears, and all sorts of wild birds which they could catch : Also bear, venison, beavers, tortoise, frogs, squirrels, dogs, skunks, rattle-snakes : Yea the very bark of trees ; besides all sorts of creatures, and provision which they plundered from the *English* : I can but stand in admiration to see the wonderful power of God, in providing for such a vast number of our enemies in the wilderness, where there was nothing to be seen, but from hand to mouth. Many times in the morning, the generality of them would eat up all they had, and yet have some farther supply against they wanted. But now our perverse and evil carriages in the sight of the Lord, have so offended him, that instead of turning his hand against them, the Lord feeds and nourishes them up to be a scourge to the whole land.

5. Another thing that I would observe is, the strange providence of God in turning things about when the *Indians* were at the highest, and the *English* at the lowest. I was with the enemy eleven weeks and five days, and not one week passed without their fury and some desolation by fire or sword upon one place or other. They mourned for their own losses, yet triumphed and rejoiced in their inhuman and devilish cruelty to the *English*. They would boast much of their victories ; saying, that in two hours time, they had destroyed such a captain and his company, in such a place ; and such a captain and his company in such a place : And boast how many towns they had destroyed, and then scoff, and say, they had done them a good turn, to send them to heaven so soon. Again they would say, this summer they would knock all the rogues on the head, or drive them into the sea, or make them fly the country ; thinking surely, *Agag* like. *The bitterness of death is past*. Now the heathen begin to think all is their own ; and the poor christians hopes fail (as to man) and now their eyes are more to God, and their hearts sigh heaven-ward, and they say in good earnest, *Help Lord, or we perish*. When the Lord had brought his people to this, that they saw no help in any thing but himself ; then he takes the quarrel into his own hand ; and tho' they had made a pit, as deep as hell for the christians that summer, yet the Lord hurled themselves into it. And the Lord had not so many ways before to preserve them, but now he hath as many to destroy them.

But to return again to my going home ; where we may see a remarkable change of providence : At first they were all against it, except my husband would come for me ; but afterward they assented to it, and seemed to rejoice in it : Some asking me to send them some bread, others some tobacco, others shaking me by the hand,

offering me a hood and scarf to ride in : Not one moving hand or tongue against it. Thus hath the Lord answered my poor desires, and the many earnest requests of others put up unto God for me. In my travels, an *Indian* came to me, and told me, if I were willing he and his Spuaw would run away, and go home along with me. I told them no, I was not willing to run away, but desired to wait God's time that I might go home quietly, and without fear. And now God hath granted me my desire. O the wonderful power of God that I have seen, and the experiences that I have had : I have been in the midst of those roaring lions, and savage bears, that feared neither God, nor man, nor the devil, by night and day, alone and in company ; sleeping all sorts together, and yet not one of them ever offered the least abuse of unchastity to me, in word or action. Though some are ready to say, I speak it for my own credit ; but I speak it in the presence of God, and to his glory. God's power is as great now, as it was to save *Daniel* in the lion's den, or the three children in the fiery furnace. Especially that I should come away in the midst of so many hundreds of enemies, and not a dog move his tongue. So I took my leave of them, and in coming along, my heart melted into tears, more than all the while I was with them, and I was almost swallowed up with the thoughts that ever I should go home again. About the sun's going down. Mr. *Hoar*, myself, and the two *Indians*, came to *Lancaster*, and a solemn sight it was to me. There had I lived many comfortable years among my relations and neighbours : and now not one christian to be seen, or one house left standing. We went on to a farm house that was yet standing, where we lay all night ; and a comfortable lodging we had, though nothing but straw to lie on. The Lord preserved us in safety that night, and raised us up again in the morning, and carried us along, that before noon we came to *Concord*. Now was I full of joy, and yet not without sorrow : Joy, to see such a lovely sight, so many christians together, and some of them my neighbours : There I met with my brother, and my brother in-law, who asked me, if I knew where his wife was ? poor heart ! he had helped to bury her, and knew it not ; she being shot down by the house, was partly burnt, so that those who were at *Boston* at the desolation of the town, came back afterward and buried the dead, did not know her. Yet I was not without sorrow, to think how many were looking and longing, and my own children among the rest, to enjoy that deliverance that I had now received ; and I did not know whether ever I should see them again. Being recruited with food and raiment, we went to *Boston* that day, where I met with my dear husband ; but the thoughts of our dear children, one being dead, and
the

the other we could not tell where, abated our comfort in each other.'
I was not before so much hem'd in by the merciless and cruel heathen, but now as much with pitiful, tender-hearted and compassionate
christians. In that poor and beggarly condition, I was received
in, I was kindly entertained in several houses: So much love I received from several (many of whom I knew not) that I am not
capable to declare it. But the Lord knows them all by name; the
Lord reward them seven fold into their bosoms of his spirituals,
for their temporals. The twenty pounds, the pirce of my redemption, was raised by some *Boston* gentlewomen, and Mr. *Usher*,
whose bounty and charity, I would not forget to make mention of.
Then Mr. *Thomas Shepard* of *Charlestown* received us into his
house, where we continued eleven weeks; and a father and mother
they were unto us. And many more tender-hearted friends we
met with in that place. We were now in the midst of love, yet
not without much and frequent heaviness of heart, for our poor
children and other relations, who were still in affliction. The
week following, after my coming in, the governor and council
sent to the *Indians* again, and that not without success; for they
brought in my sister, and goodwife *Kettle*. Their not knowing where our children were, was a sore trial to us still:
and yet we were not without secret hopes of seeing them again.
That which was dead lay heavier upon my spirits, than those
which were alive among the heathen; thinking how it suffered
with its wounds, and I was not able to relieve it, and how it was
buried by the heathen in the wilderness from among all christians.
We were hurried up and down in our thoughts, sometimes we should
hear a report that they were gone this way and sometimes that;
and that they were come in, in this place or that, we kept inquir-
ing and listening to hear concerning them, but no certain news as
yet. About this time the council had ordered a day of publick
thanksgiving, though I had still cause of mourning; and being
unsettled in our minds, we thought we would ride eastward, to see
if we could hear any thing concerning our children. As we were
riding along between *Ipswich* and *Rowley*, we met with *William
Hubbard*, who told us our son *Joseph*, and my sister's son, were
come into major *Waldren's*: I asked him how he knew it? He
said the major himself told him so. So along we went till we
came to *Newbury*; and their minister being absent, they desired
my husband to preach the thanksgiving for them; but he was not
willing to stay there that night, but he would go over to *Salisbury*,
to hear farther, and come again in the morning, which he did, and
preached there that day. At night when he had done, one came
and told him that his daughter was come into *Providence*: Here

was

was mercy on both hands. Now we were between them, the one on the east and the other on the west; our son being nearest, we went to him first, to *Portsmouth*, where we met with him, and with the major also : who told us he had done what he could, but could not redeem him under seven pounds, which the good people thereabouts were pleased to pay. The Lord reward the major, and all the rest, though unknown to me, for their labour of love. My sister's son was redeemed for four pounds, which the council gave order for the payment of. Having now received one of our children, we hastened toward the other : Going back thro' *Newbury*, my husband preached there on the Sabbath-day, for which they rewarded him manifold.

On monday we came to *Charlestown*, where we heard that the governor of *Rhode-Island* had sent over for our daughter, to take care of her, being now within his jurisdiction; which should not pass without our acknowledgments. But she being nearer *Rehoboth* than *Rhode-Island*, Mr. *Newman* went over and took care of her, and brought her to his own house. And the goodness of God was admirable to us in our low estate, in that he raised up compassionate friends on every side, when we had nothing to recompence any for their love. The *Indians* were now gone that way, that it was apprehended dangerous to go to her; but the carts which carried provision to the *English* army, being guarded, brought her with them to *Dorchester*, where we received her safe; blessed be the Lord for it. Her coming in was after this manner : She was travelling one day with the *Indians*, with her basket at her back; the company of *Indians* were got before her, and gone out of sight, all except one Squaw : She followed the Squaw till night, and then both of them lay down, having nothing over them but the heavens, nor under them but the earth. Thus she travelled three days together, having nothing to eat or drink but water and green hirtle-berries. At last they came into *Providence*, where she was kindly entertained by several of that town. The *Indians* often said, that I should never have her under twenty pounds, but now the Lord hath brought her in upon free cost, and given her to me the second time. The Lord make us a blessing indeed to each other. Thus hath the Lord brought me and mine out of that horrible pit, and hath set us in the midst of tender-hearted and compassionate christians. 'Tis the desire of my soul, that we may walk worthy of the mercies received, and which we are receiving.

Our family being now gathered together, the *South* church in *Boston* hired an house for us : Then we removed from Mr. *Shepard*'s (those cordial friends) and went to *Boston*, where we continued about three quarters of a year; still the Lord went along with us, and provided graciously for us. I thought it somewhat

strange

ſtrange to ſet up houſe-keeping with bare walls, but as *Solomon*
ſays, *money anſwers all things* : And that we had through the be-
nevolence of chriſtian friends, ſome in this town, and ſome in that,
and others ; and ſome from *England*, that in a little time we might
look and ſee the houſe furniſhed with love. The Lord hath been
exceeding good to us in our low eſtate, in that, when we had neither houſe nor home, nor other neceſſaries, the Lord ſo moved
the hearts of theſe and thoſe towards us, that we wanted neither
food nor raiment for ourſelves or ours, *Pro.* 18. 24. *There is a*
friend that ſticketh cloſer than a brother. And how many ſuch
friends have we found, and now living among us ! And truly
ſuch a friend have we found him to be unto us, in whoſe houſe we
lived, *viz.* Mr. *James Whitcomb,* a friend near hand and far off.

I can remember the time, when I uſed to ſleep quietly without
working in my thoughts, whole nights together ; but now it is
otherwiſe with me : When all are faſt about me, and no eye open,
but his who ever awaketh, my thoughts are upon things paſt, upon
the awful diſpenſations of the Lord towards us ; upon his wonderful power and might in carrying of us through ſo many difficulties,
in returning us in ſafety, and ſuffering none to hurt us. I remember in the night ſeaſon, how the other day I was in the midſt of
thouſands of enemies, and nothing but death before me : It was then
hard work to perſuade myſelf, that ever I ſhould be ſatisfied with
bread again. But now we are fed with the fineſt of the wheat
and (as I may ſay) with *honey out of the rock* : Inſtead of the
huſks we have the *fat calf* : The thoughts of theſe things in the
particulars of them, and of the love and goodneſs of God towards us
make it true of me, what *David* ſaid of himſelf, *Pſal.* 4. 6. *I*
water my couch with my tears. O the wonderful power of God that
mine eyes have ſeen, affording matter enough for my thoughts
to run in, that when others are ſleeping mine eyes are weeping.

I have ſeen the extreme vanity of this world : One hour I have
been in health, and wealth, wanting nothing, but the next hour
in ſickneſs, and wounds, and death, having nothing but ſorrow
and affliction. Before I knew what affliction meant I was ready
ſometimes to wiſh for it. When I lived in proſperity, having the
comforts of this world about me, my relations by me, and my heart
cheerful, and taking little care for any thing : and yet ſeeing many
(whom I preferred before myſelf) under many trials and afflictions,
in ſickneſs, weakneſs, poverty, loſſes, croſſes, and cares of the world,
I ſhould be ſometimes jealous leſt I ſhould have my portion in this
life, But now I ſee the Lord had his time to ſcourge and chaſten
me. The portion of ſome is to have their affliction by drops, but
the *wine of aſtoniſhment,* like a *ſweeping rain, that leaveth no food,*
did the Lord prepare to be my portion. Affliction I wanted, and

affliction

affliction I had, full meafure, preffed down and running over : Yet
I fee when God calls perfons to never fo many difficulties, yet he
is able to carry them through, and make them fay they have been
gainers thereby, and I hope I can fay, in fome meafure, as David,
t is good for me that I have been afflicted. The Lord hath
ſhewed me the vanity of thefe outward things ; that they are the
anities of vanities, and vexation of fpirit. That they are but a
ſhadow, a blaft, a bubble, and things of no continuance. If trouble
from fmaller matter begin to rife in me, I have fomething at hand
to check myfelf with, and fay, Why am I troubled ? It was but the
other day, that if I had had the world, I would have given it for my
freedom, or to have been a fervant to a chriftian. I have learned
to look beyond prefent and fmaller troubles, and to be quieted
under them, as *Mofes* faid, *Exod.* 14. 13. *Stand ftill and fee the
falvation of the Lord.*

T H E   E N D.

www.ingramcontent.com/pod-product-compliance
Lightning Source LLC
Chambersburg PA
CBHW032140080426
42733CB00008B/1141